EATING INSECTS? WHAT?!?

Western consumer perspectives

Alfredo J. Escribano Ph.D., MBA

Copyright © 2020 Alfredo Jesus Escribano Sanchez

All rights reserved

No part of this book may be reproduced, or stored in a retrieval system, or transmitted in any form or by any means, electronic, mechanical, photocopying, recording, or otherwise, without express written permission of the author.

ASIN: B088RJZXCV

COVER IMAGE

Metaphor: mental image of how a Western consumer might feel like when putting insects in his/her mouth

CONTENTS

Title Page
Copyright
COVER IMAGE
Foreword
1. WESTERN CONSUMER PERSPECTIVES   4
2. rEGULATORY PILLS   16
About The Author   20

FOREWORD

SUMMARY

Foods of animal origin are, with controversy, increasingly being associated by consumers with greenhouse gas emissions, pollution, resources depletion, ethics, and health issues. This, along with the increasing global population and the limited resources has led to a search for new sources of food. **Insects as food** is a trendy topic in this sense. However, most consumers (at least in Western societies) are reluctant to include them in their diets.

This book **summarizes knowledge about Western consumer perceptions** aiming to (1) be useful to the food industry and (2) informative for curious and concerned consumers.

NOTE

I make no pretense to this book being adapted to formal requisites such as featuring an exhaustive review, being perfectly written, or other formal aspects. I prefer for the book to provide useful tidbits of information that (1) allow both consumers and industry to acquire knowledge about the topic and (2) enable hungry readers (including food product developers) to reach for hard data after this introductory book.

1. WESTERN CONSUMER PERSPECTIVES

Factors To Consider For Developing Insect-Based Foods In The West

People throughout the world have been eating insects as a regular part of their diets for millennia, in different ethnic groups and in different countries, namely Asia, Africa, Mexico and South America. According to the UN Food and Agriculture Organization, at least 2 billion people, particularly in Asian countries such as Thailand and Vietnam, already regularly consume insects.

However, in Western societies, entomophagy is uncommon, even a taboo or joke.

From a scientific point of view, this rejection is not logical as insects share many characteristics with crustaceans, which are a delicacy for many of us, such as lobsters, a sea-insect.

Looking at the future, some say that insects are tipped to be a sushi rival as fashionable food.

In terms of regulation recently regulated the use of insects for human consumption. However, the distance between legal allowance and consumers' willingness to eat. Different factors, discussed below, influence this Western reluctance to eat insects.

1. BELIEFS and ATTITUDES toward insects

Food neophobia is the main challenge to insects consumption: a one-unit increase in the food neophobia score was associated with an 84% decrease in the predicted odds of being ready to adopt insects (Verbeke, 2015).

In this sense, although there is an increasing interest toward insects as an alternative protein source in Western countries, so far, most Western consumers react with **disgust** and **rejection**.

2. INFORMATION, RATIONAL CHOICES & COMMUNICATION STRATEGIES

In an attempt to reduce food neophobia, providing information has been shown to be key.

In fact, people with previous **entomophagy experience give higher ratings to eating insects**, meaning that **insect tasting sessions** are important to decrease food neophobia, as they encourage people to "take the first step" and become acquainted with entomophagy. From the industry/stores point of view, tastings would be then a strategic tool to reduce both neophobia and **the difference between expectations and the real experience of eating insects**.

Literature indicates that in the development and marketing of insect food, **generating positive emotional expectations key. Therefore, eliminating initial negative expectations of disgust are not enough.** You, product developer, surprise consumers with a great recipe and tasting sessions, involve top Chefs!

A good example of the positive effect of these initiatiatives was the Eating Insects Conference and Tasting Demonstration organized by San Diego State University in 2019. The event consisted of an educational session that provided information about entomophagy followed by a cooking and tasting demonstration. Surveys were conducted before and after the event in order to assess the its effect on participants' acceptance of entomophagy. The higher knowledge of participants after attending the event increased their willingness to consume edible insects. Participants who believed that entomophagy is sustainable were more willing to consume edible insects than those who did not. Moreover, those participants with previous consumption experiences had higher post-event willingness to consume insects, indicating that exposure is positive to reduce the cultural and knowledge barrier of Western consumers about eating insects.

What kind of information?

Communication has a significant effect on eating behavior. Including mesages about the benefits (e.g. health or environmental) of eating insects has a positive impact, especially **societal mes-**

sages; these appeared to be more robust over time.

Marketing / communication strategies with long-lasting effects on consumers: e.g. messages about social **benefits**, such as health and environment, in case it is proven. It is not possible to generalize (insects vs. meat) due to the huge variety of insects species and livestock production systems and their externalities. The solution would be to carry out (too many) **comparisons of apples to apples**, as is done with regular and light chips. Is this feasible?

However, **arguments about environmental or nutritional benefits are not sufficient** to shift people's choices toward entomophagy. Different factors such as country culture and values, gender, and previous knowledge about the topic must be taken into account when designing our communication strategies and campaigns. In line with this, Hoek et al. (2011) pointed out that efforts must be made to significantly improve the **sensory quality** and **resemblance to meat**. However, the approach of meat substitution seems to be not correct as insects will be an additional ingredient, not a substitute one.

Nutritional composition is information, a rational factor, and a major motivator. This book does not address this topic. More information can be found about this topic in the review of Kourimska & Adamkova (2016), among other studies.

Not all consumers should be approached with the same communication/advertisement strategies/campaigns. Other traditional **marketing mix** Ps (price and promotion) cannot be neglected. In this sense, it is interesting to mention the study by Clarkson et al. (2018), exploring 32 consumers' attitudes, drivers, and barriers towards entomophagy aimed to uncover consumer expectations surrounding what their ideal **insect product attributes**. Designs included the ideal product, place, price, and promotional attributes. Common barriers were culture, food neophobia, disgust sensitivity, lack of necessity, and knowledge. Motivational drivers were novelty, health, sustainability, and/or nutrition (Clarkson et al., 2018).

3. SENSORY QUALITY

Sensory quality is basic for the acceptance of any kind of food. This is even more important for novel ones.

Texture becomes key during the experience of eating certain insects, as they many times hard, crunchy, have long legs, etc. This along with their aspect are part of the famous *"yuk" effect*. In other cases (larvae), the experience may be quite the opposite: a pasty product.

For example, in cookies with mealworms, taste attracted the most positive attitude towards the cookie and also generated the most customer willingness to try. This was followed by texture (crunchiness).

However, insect **tastes** and **flavors** are quite diverse and these sensory properties depend, among other aspects, on the environment where insects lived and the feed they ate. This supports the above statement that a controlled environment seems more suitable in order to control quality standardization. In this sense, the selection of feed can also be adapted depending on how we want the insects to taste. If insects are scalded, they are practically tasteless, because pheromones are washed off by rinsing. During cooking, insects take the flavor of added ingredients.

Regarding **color**, product developers must consider how insects change after every single cooking process. Thus, appealing colors may become disgusting ones after either boiling or frying. A pleasing color does not always indicate that an insect is tasty. During cooking, the insect's color usually changes from the original shades of grey, blue, or green to red (Ramos-Elorduy, 1998). Insects containing a considerable amount of oxidized fat, or improperly dried insects, may become black after cooking.

However, **sensory-liking is necessary but insufficient for novel food acceptance**, including for insects. Sensorially-driven strategies such as changes in name and **visual presentation** can change people's expectations.

A key topic: **whole, bits, or flour?**

Cavallo and Materia (2018) stated that **the most powerful driver for insect consumption** among Italian Millennials **can be the invisibility of the insect's shape.** This is one of the main barriers and points to be taken into account when developing food products with insects, as *ensuring that insects are not visible will increase the willingness to eat insects* (Lombardi et al. 2019).

Therefore, carriers (e.g. pasta, cookies, etc.) used as well as their form (powder, liquid, oil) will generate different results in terms of willingness to pay (WTP) for insect-based versions of the products.

Insect integration into Western food culture will take time and must be donde following different steps from minced or powdered insects, as consumers are not ready to add whole insects to their diets. If we think about potential products to develop, it seems that snacks containing insects are not a good idea.

Whole insects alone, or even products containing bits, are more preferable to mixed snacks (Gmuer et al., 2016).

4. PREVIOUS EXPERIENCES, FAMILIARITY, EXPOSURE, and APPROPRIATENESS

Decades of laboratory research, as well as years of experience in gastronomy, indicate that **people's food choices tend to be driven by taste preferences and exposure** (related to familiarity and appropriateness).

Unusual novel foods have low sensory appeal mainly due to low food appropriateness so that **insects should be included as part of familiar products** in order to improve not only the sensory quality and initial sensory expectations, but also to make meals containing insects more appropriate (Tan et al., 2017).

The **food industry should start with advertising campaigns in order to speed up the familiarity process**. In this regard, supermarkets should be open to hearing about insects and consider **setting up at least small insect areas (despite zero consumption) in order to increase product exposure, availability, and then familiarity**. Products must be culturally accepted in order to be appropriate. An example would be bakery products containing insect flour. However, regulations must cover insects flour, which is not yet considered nowadays in many countries.

Tan et al. (2016) showed the importance of **previous communication** and the effect of **having a pleasant experience** (linked to food appropriateness: burger) with novel foods in order to increase their acceptance. They concluded that positive sensory experiences play a role in the process of accepting a food, but food **appropriateness** is also needed, and the latter is the factor that **predicts repeated consumption**.

However, appropriateness alone is not sufficient, nor is familiarity neither. In this sense, Tan et al. (2017) concluded that appropriate **product design** is important but insufficient to achieve consumer acceptance of insects as food in the West. Additional incentives are required to encourage acceptance beyond the mere willingness to try.

The difficulty is the combination of so many factors so that high product **acceptability was not simply achieved by adding mealworms to familiar foods.**, and again, one of the most important topics is the **appropriateness of the product combination**.

In line with this, the study by Gmuer et al. (2016) shows how **lack of familiarity explains why snacks containing insects are still far from being on a par with well-established products** in a Western country (Switzerland). Consumers visualized images of the products differing in their degree of the insect ingredient processing: tortilla chips made with cricket flour ("flour"), tortilla chips containing deep-fried cricket bits ("bits"), a snack consisting of tortilla chips and deep-fried crickets ("mix"), and deep-fried crickets ("crickets"). This study showed not only expectations of disgust from respondents, but also that the **insect snacks evoked various negative emotional expectations** that went beyond mere disgust.

5. THE CONTEXT

The importance of the commercial context where the insects are sold is a driver of entomophagous practices (Sidali et al. 2019). These authors suggested that the **introduction of contextual cultural information** about insects as a food source may help to preclude a priori false assumptions regarding entomophagy. Recipes and tastes that are part of local cuisine will make the introduction of insects easier. In line with this, Tan el at. (2017) mentioned that insect-based foods should **meet the taste standards of the product category**.

The social context (feeling of social belonging and status) influence the adoption of goods and habits, which include foods.

6. SOCIAL AND CULTURAL NORMS

Another barrier is the lack of social norms related to entomophagy in the West. **Cultural norms** in Western countries view entomophagy **as a disgusting practice** (Myers & Pettigrew, 2018). Insects eating norm emerged as a significant predictor of insect tasting behavior. These findings suggest that perceived social norms play a substantial role in Westerners' (un)willingness to eat insects. The result gives reason for optimism regarding the aspirations of introducing insects in Western food diet and point to avenues for **harnessing social norms in marketing efforts** (Jensen & Lieberoth, 2019).

7. AVAILABILITY AND CONVENIENCE

Availability in stores will increase **exposure** and **familiarity**.

Furthermore, availability and **convenience** are key given (1) current consumer behavior related to impatience and the perceived lack of time (*I want it now!*), and (2) the low willingness to spend time on housework. A stronger convenience orientation in food choice (a unit increase) increases the likelihood of adopting insects by 75% (Verbeke, 2015).

Consumers are craving convenience, longing for the ease taken for granted before daily habits were upended (Euromonitor International, 2021).

8. INITIAL TRYING vs. REPEATED CONSUMPTION

House (2016) distinguished between initial motivations and repeat consumption factors. While factors **affecting repeat consumption are highly conventional** (e.g. price, taste, availability, and the degree to which they match current eating habits), **initial motivations (initial trying) are diverse and depend on consumer profiles.** People tended to be prompted either by curiosity or by rationalized principles such as ethics (e.g. a desire to reduce the environmental impact of their diets and animal welfare). Of course, taste is essential increasing repeated consumption.

Sogari et al. (2017) researched the reasons to try through the study of the expectations about entomophagy from a specific target group (foodies) composed by people studying Gastronomy and Food Science. The study was held at the University of Parma (Italy) in April 2015 and consisted of a student engagement with a so-called "bug banquet" with a cookie made using "insect flour". Results showed that almost all the students tasted the product and were willing to try other edible insects in the future. **Curiosity was the most important reason to choose to try** the cookie made with cricket flour; whereas **negative opinions** from family members and friends (social and cultural norms) and the disgust factor may prevent Western consumers from eating insects in the future.

Tan et al. (2017) explored differences between individuals who differed (willing, n = 135; vs. unwilling tasters, n = 79) in their intentions/motivations to eat appropriate (i.e. meatball) and inappropriate (i.e. dairy drink) mealworm products along with the original mealworm-free products. These authors gave an important recommendation to the industry: future research should **not only put emphasis on increasing initial motivations to try but should address the barriers to buying and preparing insects for regular consumption**.

Little attention has been given to understanding how more appealing products could be developed, and whether that is sufficient to encourage consumption of culturally unusual food, as **even with high interest and good products**, willing consumers **still hesitate to consume insect-based foods regularly due to other practical and socio-cultural factors** (Tan et al., 2017).

9. SAFETY and INFECTABILITY

As recently found by Euromonitor International (2021), Safety Obsessed is the new wellness movement. The fear of infection and increased health awareness drive demand.

In the case of insects, perceived infectability does not predict insect-disgust or willingness to eat insects (Jensen & Lieberoth, 2019). Despite this is an important topic, it seems it is not among the main ones for consumers. These authors tested the effects of contamination fear and perceived social eating norms with a survey sample of Danish college students (N = 189). Self-reported trait-level Pathogen Disgust and Perceived Infectability did not consistently predict insect eating disgust or willingness to eat insects.

My thought and doubt in this regard is that the yuk/disgust could be unconsciously including, in some cases, not only the emotion related to aspect and texture but also to safety?

10. CONSUMERS PROFILES

Early adopters, rather than the population at large, should receive greater analytic attention at this stage in which insects are still novel foods in Western countries (House, 2016).

The Barclays report mentioned that members of Generation Z are the "most likely to overcome the 'yuck factor' associated with consuming insects", due to their interest on health and sustainability.

Frequency and/or attachment to meat consumption and the consumer's level of environmental concern are related to consumer's willingnes to carry out a partial change in their diets from meat to insects. Information given about the environmental impact and sustainability of food choices increase the likelihood of adopting more sustainable foods by 71% per sustainability unit increase (Verbeke, 2015).

Consumers demand that companies care beyond revenue, and they no longer perceive businesses as profit-driven entities. Protecting the health and interest of society and the planet is the new expectation. Companies should help reshape the world in a more sustainable way (Euromonitor International, 2021).

Regarding gender, males are more likely than females to adopt insects (Verbeke, 2015). Caparros Megido et al. (2016) found that gender influenced participants' overall liking of hybrid insect-based burgers (made of beef, lentils, mealworms and beef, and mealworms and lentils) in addition to burger appearance and taste. Men seem less neophobic than women as they were less influenced by the burger's appearance.

Finally, the effects of distinct types of knowledge differ between Northern and Central Europe, and Northern Europe might currently be a better market area for insect food.

11. PRICE

Price, in line with sensory profile, is a key attribute in food choices. Insects and products containing insects must be appropriate to the product line.

In this sense, prices still remain high, but it is expected that this situation will change once insect farming and the whole agri-food chain mature and evolves in terms of volume (economy of scale), structure and efficiency.

2. REGULATORY PILLS

European Regulatory Pills

Legal rules on the use of insects as feed and food vary across the world. In the case of the European Union, animals farming operations must ensure animal health (EU Animal Health Law': Regulation (EU) No 2016/429 on transmissible animal diseases) and EU environmental legislation (Regulation EU No 1143/2014: restricts the insect species that are eligible for farming purposes).

When it comes to food safety, any operator must comply with the 'General Food Law' (Regulation No 178/2002) and the 'Hygiene Package' (e.g. Regulation No 852/2004 on the hygiene of foodstuffs and Regulation No 183/2005 laying down requirements for feed hygiene).

In addition to the 'general food hygiene requirements', the production and marketing of insects as food in Europe is governed by the 'Novel Foods' legislation – i.e. Regulation (EU) No 2015/2283. At the beginning of 2021, still no insect species has been authorised on the EU market. However, on the basis of the first EFSA opinion covering an insect species (January 2021), the first authorisation could take place in mid-2021 (IPIFF, 2021).

However, insects regulation has been more complex. There was an absence of legal certainty regarding the scope of the "old" novel food legislation (Regulation (EC) No 258/97, which was repealed on 1 January 2018 by Regulation EU 2015/2283), and therefore, the placement on the market of certain whole insects for human consumption was tolerated. This only concerned insects belonging to ten species for which food safety had been evaluated in a 'common advice' document from the Scientific Committee of the FASFC and the Superior Health Council.

Such uncertainty regarding the scope of Regulation (EC) No 258/97 was removed in October 2020 as whole insects were not considered to be "novel food" under Regulation (EC) No 258/97 (Case C-526/19).

This led to the application of the transitional measures provided for in paragraph 2 of Article 35 Regulation (EU) No 2015/2283.

On May 3rd , EU Member States' delegates in the EU Standing Committee on Plants, Animals, Food and Feed have backed a draft Commission Implementing Regulation, aiming at authorising the placing on the EU market of dried Tenebrio molitor larvae, based on a novel food application submitted by the French insect producer SAS EAP Group Agronutris. This positive vote follows the recent publication by the European Food Safety Authority (EFSA) of a scientific opinion which concluded that such product is safe, in accordance with the conditions of use and specifications proposed by the abovementioned applicant (IPIFF, 2021).

SUMMARY AND RECOMMENDATIONS

The adoption of insects as food by Western consumers seems more likely to succeed if insects are processed and incorporated into familiar foods (Hartmann et al., 2015).

Exposure to the product will make insects more familiar and will reduce cultural barriers and the lack of appropriateness.

The information provided will influence consumer decisions but the rational brain is not leading the decision making process alone.

Expectations can be modulated by such information and must be done in order to reduce differences between expectations and the real experience of eating insects. In this sense, strategies must be designed to achieve a repeated consumption (vs. initial trying).

Sensory quality is a must, but it is not enough, the appropriateness of the insect ingredient must be considered, which depends on the commercial context and cultural norms.

On the basis of consumer profile, different strategies must be developed too: mention the sustainability benefits of eating insects vs. other foods to environmentally-concerned, similar to health-concerned consumers, use influencers and record videos in popular social networks to approach young generations, or invite the best Chefs to attract foodies.

ABOUT THE AUTHOR

Alfredo J. Escribano

Dr. Alfredo J. Escribano is from Cáceres, Extremadura, Spain, where he grew up in the region that is home to the famous Iberian pigs. This semi-arid area boasts high cultural and environmental value, and the agri-food sector is key for its population.

His Ph.D. work focused on the sustainability of organic and conventional beef cattle farms, with a strong vision of farm economics.

He is also Master on Meat Science, MBA, and has education on Agri-Food Marketing, among other topics related to business.

Alfredo has worked in various positions within the animal feed industry.

He is also independent researcher, consultant, and writer focused on agri-food sustainability and consumer behavior towards foods.

Moreover, he contributes to different scientific/Academic and industry entities.

Alfredo has published numerous peer-reviewed publications, scientific and industry talks, industry magazine articles, and book chapters. He has delivered invited presentations around the world primarily on the sustainability of animal production systems and animal nutrition.

www.ingramcontent.com/pod-product-compliance
Lightning Source LLC
Chambersburg PA
CBHW040347220526
45473CB00009B/2808